# My Family, Your Family
# mi familia, tu familia

written by Sam Tura Probadora
illustrated by Berna Rode
translated by Mercedes Palacio

www.samtprobadora.com

Mama, Papa, & Jericho – My Ohana. Thank you for your unconditional love, support, and sacrifice.

Warren & Sharon – Our family is forever changed because of you. Thank you.

Colin – Thank you for listening to my countless stories and encouraging me to pursue my dreams.

To my students and families – Thank you for your courage. You stories inspire me.

To my friends and colleagues whose hearts and advocacy continue to teach with love and hope – You are a light this world needs.

ISBN: 9780578853482
Library of Congress Number: 2021908817

First Hardcover Printing Edition: 2021

Written by © Samantha Tura Probadora
Cover art by © Berna Rode
Layout and Book Design by © Samantha Tura Probadora

Printed by Village Books in the United States of America.

www.samtprobadora.com

"What makes your family special?"
my teacher asked.

"¿Qué hace especial a tu familia?"
preguntó mi maestra.

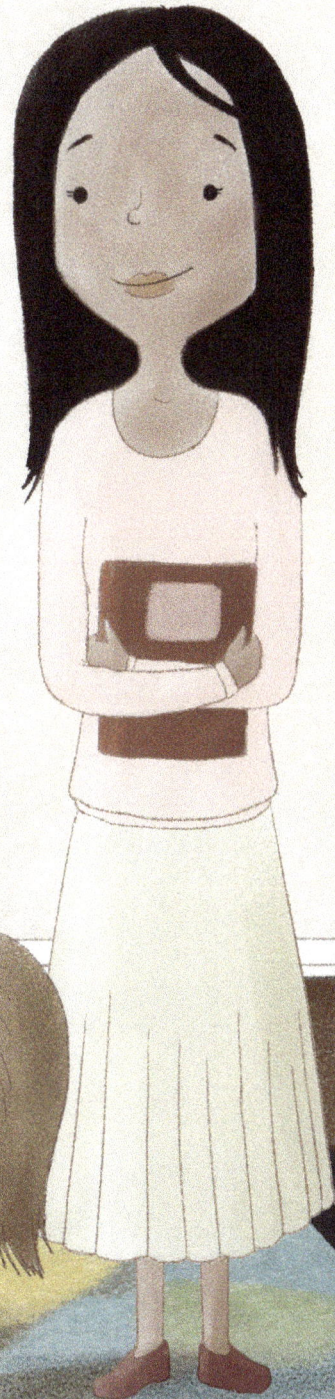

"My family is different. We are not like everybody else's family." So, I turned off my camera and shared last.

"Mi familia es diferente. No somos como el resto de las familias."
Así que, apagué me cámara y fui el último en compartir.

"I live with my dad and grandmother. Some people think she's my mom. She's not. Grandma and Dad are my everything!"

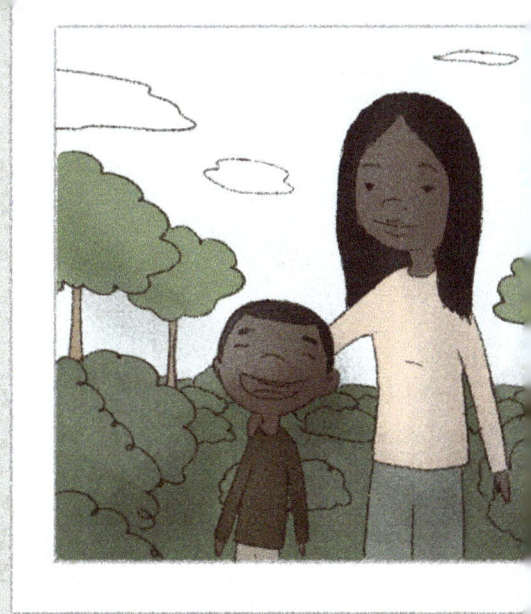

"Vivo con mi Papá y mi abuela. Algunas personas creen que ella es mi mamá. Pero no es. ¡La abuela y Papá son mi todo!"

"My brother and I lived with many families before we met mom and dad. I love going on hikes with my family."

"Mi hermano y yo vivimos con muchas familias antes de conocer a mamá y papá. Me encanta ir de excursión con mi familia."

"Both my dads like to sing. They are not the best singers, but they give the best hugs."

"A mis papás les encanta cantar.
No son los mejores cantantes,
pero dan los mejores abrazos."

"I love dinner time with my big family. Mama and Papa make the best hummus and falafel."

"Me encanta la hora de la cena
con mi familia. Mamá y Papá
hacen el mejor hummus y falafel."

"We all look alike in my family.
We just kind of go together."

"Todos nos parecemos en mi familia.
Es como que quedamos bien juntos."

"We live with Mom most of the time. Other times,
we live with Dad. I think it's fair."

"Vivimos con Mamá la mayor parte del tiempo.
Otras veces, vivimos con Papá. Creo que es justo."

"My family likes to pick apples together. Some say I look like Dad. Some say I look like Mom. I think I look like me!"

"A mi y a mi familia nos encanta recolectar manzanas juntos. Algunos dicen que me veo como papá. Otros dicen que me veo como mamá. ¡Yo creo que me veo como yo!"

"Our mom always says that two are better than one! We love painting with mom, especially when dad brings us snacks."

"Nuestra mamá siempre dice que dos son mejor que una! Nos encanta patinar con mamá, especialmente cuando papá nos trae bocadillos."

"We have a new baby in our house. I'm not quite sure how I feel about him. I wonder if they can take him back."

"Tenemos un nuevo bebe en casa. No estoy seguro de cómo me siento con él. Me pregunto si podrán devolverlo."

"Dad is my best friend. I love spending time with him. We like to go on bike rides. But my favorite thing is beating him in basketball."

"Papá es mi mejor amigo. Me encanta pasar tiempo con él. Nos gusta hacer recorridos en bici. Pero mi cosa favorita es ganarle en el basket".

"One of my moms has dark hair. My other mom has blonde hair, just like me! We love rollerblading and going on bike rides together."

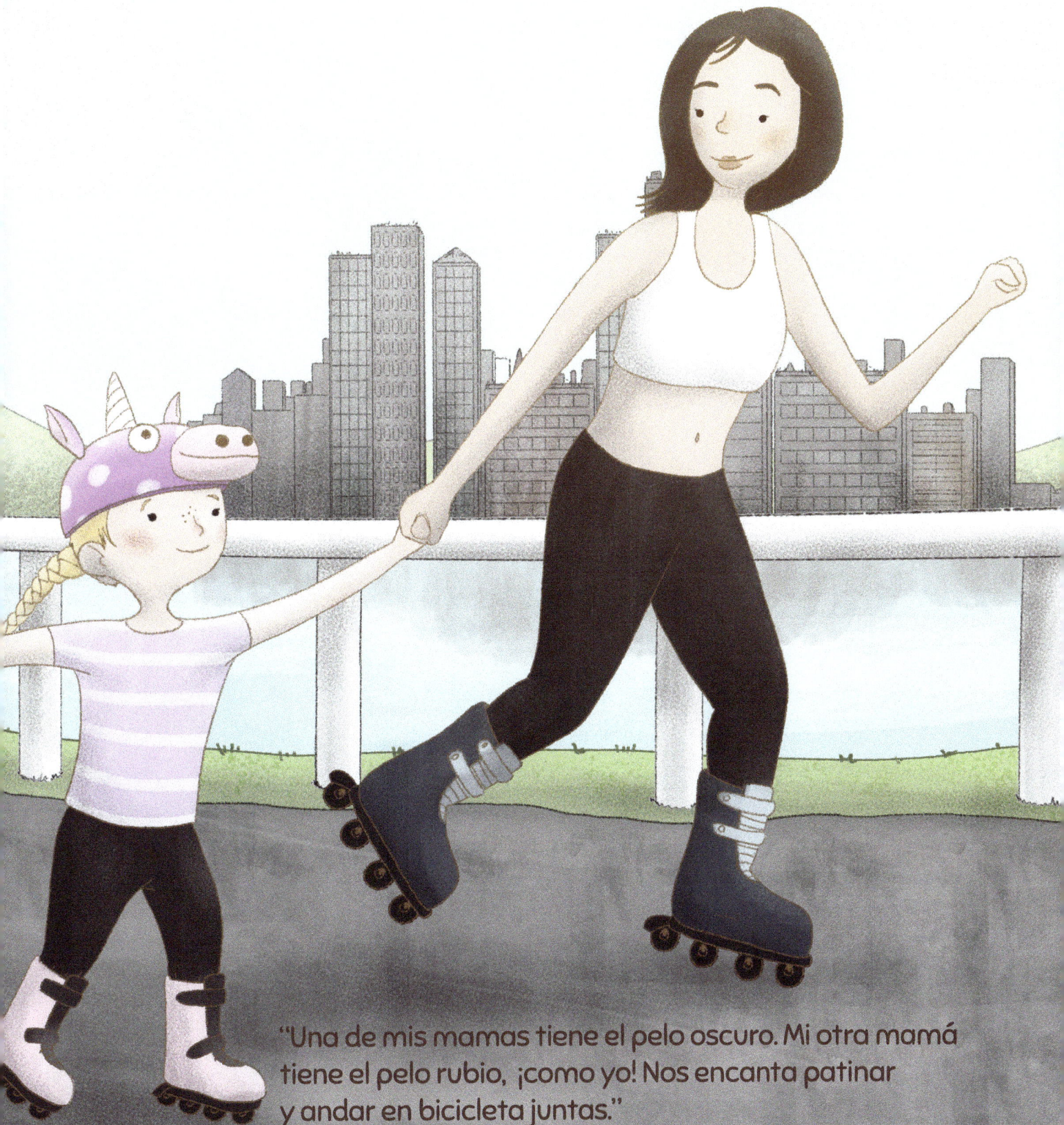

"Una de mis mamas tiene el pelo oscuro. Mi otra mamá tiene el pelo rubio, ¡como yo! Nos encanta patinar y andar en bicicleta juntas."

"There are lots of kids in our family. Some are little. Some are big. Mom and Dad just keep coming home with more."

"Hay un montón de niños en nuestra familia. Algunos son pequeños. Algunos son grandes. Mamá y Papá siguen llegando a casa con más."

"My mama and papa have been friends since they were small like me. Now we are a family. We are the best of friends!"

"Mi mamá y mi papá han sido amigos desde que eran pequeños como yo. Ahora somos una familia. ¡Somos los mejores amigos!"

"People say I look like my mom. I think so too.
I have brown hair, just like her!"

"Hay gente que dice que me veo como mi mamá. Yo también lo creo.
¡Tengo el pelo marrón, igual que ella!"

"While I listened to everybody talk about their families,
I remembered something that made my family special."

"Mientras escuchaba a todos hablar sobre sus familias,
me acordé de algo que hace especial a mi familia."

"We were at the bike park one day. A lady asked Mom and Dad if we were their real children. "Oh, we don't have imaginary kids," Mom said. "Both our children are real! We are a real family."

"Un día estábamos en el parque de bicis. Una señora le preguntó a mamá y papá si éramos sus hijos reales. "Oh, no tenemos hijos imaginarios", dijo mamá. "¡Nuestros dos hijos son reales! Somos una familia real."

"What makes your family special?"

"¿Qué hace especial a tu familia?"

# My Family – mi familia

Draw your family. Dibuja a tu familia.

# FAMILY – INCLUSIVE LANGUAGE

Use: "grownup" "adult" "caregiver"
Avoid: "parents" "mom" "dad" "mom and dad"
Why? Includes children who may not have parents and other children accompanied by other adults other than a parent. These adults may include: grandparents, step-parents, and other adult roles.

Use: "family"
Avoid: "extended family"
Why? Includes grandparents, aunts, uncles, and cousins – for many cultures

Use: "family members"
Avoid: "members of a household'
Why? Includes families that live outside of a household. For example, families with children and adults that live in different countries, cities, and household; families with divorced or incarcerated caregivers.

Use: "children"
Avoid: "son" "daughter" "brother" "sister"
Why? Includes grandchildren, nieces, nephews, godchildren, gender queer children, foster children, and adopted children.

## PRE-READING QUESTIONS

- When you think of family, who do you think of? (People you live with and those far away, people you may or may not be related to).
- What makes a family? Are families all the same or different?
- Who do you live with? Who are the adults in your home? Do you live with other children?
- Families come in all shapes, colors, and sizes, but there is one thing they all have in common. What do you think that might be?

## POST-READING QUESTIONS

- What makes a family special? What makes your family special?
- What do you love most about your family?
- How is your family alike and different from other families?
- After reading the book, how did you idea about families change?
- Let's learn about each other's families. What did you learn about other families?
- How can we learn about other families?
- What does your family have in common with families in the book?

# Author's Afterword

First Day of School – 2001

Coming to America – 2001

My family and I immigrated to the United States as refugees when I was 12. I have spent the latter half of my life yearning for a sense of belonging. I struggled to find communities who accepted me and my family as Filipinx immigrants, who walked between two cultures. As a child, I often felt alone and misunderstood.

Growing up with my brother, Jericho, we loved reading and often found refuge in children's picture books. This love became a double-edged sword; a painful reminder of how different my family looked to many. Our brownness and non-traditional family structure often resulted people treating us differently.

Reflecting on this, fills me with unimaginable anguish. I yearn to reach out to that little brown girl and those like her who feel alienated and isolated. I distinctly recall knowing that I had to prove my intellect to others from fifth grade onward. I vowed to exceed all expectations of me and my family whenever and however I could.

This book has been the culmination of my journey as a daughter and sister of Filipinx immigrants, as well as a culturally responsive educator who longed to walk into a classroom and open a book; a book with characters who looked like me.

Through this book, I hope that students of all shades of brown are honored; that families, communities, and educators grow, engage, dream, and achieve a better world for all of our children.

–Samantha Tura Probadora, Author

## About Sam Tura Probadora

Sam writes her first book, My Family, Your Family – mi familia, tu familia, dedicated to children and adults who are disproportionately underrepresented in children's literature. Through her passion of culturally responsive education, she hopes to promote the love of reading through culturally diverse and inclusive materials.

Sam immigrated from the Philippines with her family at the age of 12, finding refuge in the United States. Sam and her brother sought after children's picture books for comfort, only to be reminded the world they now called "home" often came with a price – while being marginalized and misunderstood.

Author – Som Tura Probadora

Since then, she has become an advocate for underrepresented children and family, a sought-after speaker, presenting at schools and conferences, educating students, parents, and educators on culturally responsive practice, diversity, and inclusion.

## About Berna Rode and Mercedes Palacio

Berna's love and passion for drawing started as a child. Creating illustrations that instill love in drawings and literacy fulfills his life calling. Berna is also passionate about creating animation – finding inspiration from Ghilbi and Pixar Studios.

Michi, translator, has a background in educational science and is passionate about education. She dreams of a brighter and inclusive future for many children around the world. As a translator, Michi believes in the power of language – through language we can honor different cultures and bring people together.

Illustrator – Berna Rode
Translator – Mercedes Palacio

Berna and Michi are currently based in Argentina, with their fur babies. Similar passions like food, photography, and traveling has brought Berna and Michi's paths together.